First Published in 1993
PCCS BOOKS
3 Chelford Rd
Old Trafford
Manchester
M16 0BJ

An Incomplete Guide to Referral Issues for Counsellors

ISBN   1 898059 01 0

Cover Design by Peter Kneebone
Printed by Printoff Graphic Arts Ltd. Alexander House,
Lomeshaye Road, Nelson, Lancashire

Contents

Contents

Introduction

During January 1991 I was working in Germany with British youth workers attached to the British Army on the Rhine. I had been working with two colleagues delivering an intensive, four-day, bereavement counselling skills course in preparation for the gulf war, and on the last day I was leading a large group session on 'referring on'. It occurred to me that this was a difficult session to deliver as the aims of the session were to help course members understand areas of counselling skills work where they might need to consider referral, without undermining their (recently constructed) confidence in their use of counselling skills or implying that referral should be done in a 'pseudo-professional' sort of way.

I realised that referring on clients that have been receiving counselling skills or have been involved in discreet, structured counselling relationships is a complex, subtle and skilled activity that is often not given a tight focus in counselling texts and training courses. Hopefully, this book will contribute to helping counsellors and counselling skills users improve on their sensitivity, skilfulness and professionalism with which we make such referrals.

Steve Williams
Manchester
1993

1 What is Referral?

At first or even second glance, the title of this chapter might seem like an insultingly simplistic question. This book is an attempt to raise the various issues associated with counselling referrals. The message is 'be prepared' for that moment when you wonder whether your client wants a different, possibly specialist, counsellor or you think you can't cope with the things your client is bringing to the counselling session or the phone rings and a stranger announces themselves as the counsellor at some distant university asking if you'll see their client over the summer vacation. Decisions at such times are often made 'on-the-hoof'. There are also those times when our feelings are touched, for example if a client makes a 'self-onward-referral' by just never returning or walking out on us. It's then that your client, you, your supervisor and the person to whom your client was referred are all left to pick up the pieces.

Firstly, we might like to take time to consider where referral is located in the range of helping activities. Do we consider it to be a central counselling skill or does it lie in the helping margins somewhere between 'information giving' and 'advocacy'? By 'information giving' and advocacy' I mean, do we think that referral consists of either handing out a leaflet detailing local specialist services, or taking our clients along personally to help them with their benefits claim?

Secondly, it would be too easy to dismiss referral as a lightweight 'mechanical' issue that an experienced counsellor can handle like falling off a log. All of the decisions we as counsellors make, tell us something about ourselves and now perhaps we could consider what lies behind the referral process for us as individuals.

The main argument in the book is that making referrals is a principled, skilled, ethically driven activity which needs to be actively developed by all helpers through both training and supervision. It may help to imagine a sort of 'referral checklist' of things to do before making (or receiving) a referral. The checklist would raise our awareness of the possible hidden forces directing us to make decisions, sometimes by default, sometimes because we didn't bother to check things out, or sometimes because we just didn't think.

A personal checklist might look something like this:

• Where does the 'energy' or 'need' for the referral come from?
  Does it come from me or my client?
  Is the client seeking different, more specialised help?
  Have I reached the limit of my competence?

• What is my aim for the referral?

• Can I make this referral so that the client's life and experience is added to rather than taken away from, and so that they experience it as positive and affirming rather than negative and rejecting?

• What do I want to say to my client?

• What supervision issues does it raise for me?
  What are my feelings about the client?
  Do I feel rejected or a failure?

Helpers of all complexions and levels of skill will make referrals as part of their helping regardless of their training or competence. Skilled, ethical referral is also free from the clutter of arguments over theoretical orientation. So whatever the training in helping skills that we received was called, be it 'listening skills', 'non-directive counselling', 'person-centred (Rogerian)', 'cognitive behavioural' or whatever, we should all be aware of and committed to making skilled principled referrals.

This book is structured in such a way as to raise these issues, present some options and ask some questions to help the reader build their own ethical framework of skilled referral decisions.

6 Referral Issues for Counsellors

2 Why Should You Refer On?

Because of you   1) Your personal limits

2) Your professional limits

3) The limits of your competence

Because of the client   4) The client needs a package of care involving counselling

5) The client needs another kind of counsellor

6) The client needs other kinds of care

Because of your agency 7) Time limits

8) Types of service offered

9) Policies

Because of you

1) Your personal limits.

As professional counsellors and volunteers alike, we work in an intimate way with individuals in varying degrees of distress. Our training and philosophies usually revolve around meeting our clients in an authentic, human way, with as few barriers to real contact as possible. Most of us have worked hard on our self-awareness and personal development to enable us not to get in the way of our clients' work. However, every day we hear of the things that have happened to our clients and we sometimes fear that the same things may happen to us. Despite our training, development and experience we are, above all, still human and therefore vulnerable.

The most useful thing for us to do to help our clients and ourselves is to recognise our own vulnerability and find ways of expressing and dealing with our own feelings and concerns. This is so obvious it doesn't need stating - or does it? Many of us working in the counselling field come from other professional backgrounds where we are almost always encouraged to behave as though we were invincible and can somehow remain unaffected by the people we work with.

I remember seeing a TV play in which a patient had recently died in a hospital setting. Two nurses had just completed last offices for the dead person, effectively one of the last caring acts you can perform for a person you have been involved in caring for. Both nurses had established a strong relationship with the person who had died and yet minutes after performing the last offices the more senior of the two nurses reminded the other that they "must get on.....nurses are concerned with the living not the dead." The idea that we can get close to the suffering of other human beings and remain unaffected by either their suffering, or the echoes of this in our own lives, is a damaging one for us and for our clients.

It follows therefore that sometimes we may need to consider asking a colleague to work with a client where, for example, their concerns are very close to an unresolved concern of our own. Loss and grief are clear examples of such a situation. It is a measure of the competency of the counsellor to track their own feelings and concerns accurately so that they have a good awareness of their personal limits.

There is a fine line to tread between accurate self-awareness and a hypochondriacal over sensitivity towards your own issues. It is always a good idea to
• check any areas of doubt with a supervisor and
• realise that major life events can knock you off balance, e.g. a loss or transition such as bereavement, redundancy or separation.

In Training : List all of the different ways a counsellor can gather awareness of their own 'tender spots' which may limit their work with clients.

---

2) Your professional limits.

You may be using counselling skills to enhance your primary role as a teacher, youth worker, social worker, etc. and I imagine the majority of readers of this text will be in such a situation. This is a perfectly legitimate and ethical use of counselling skills recognised by the British Association of Counselling in the document 'The Code of Ethics and Practice for Counselling Skills'. However, just because it's recognised and ethical doesn't mean it's always easy, or even possible.

One of the problems that can occur if you are using counselling skills in this way is that you can feel pulled in two directions by the demands made upon you by your primary professional role on the one hand and your desire to offer the best possible counselling on the other. Sometimes this is described as *role tension* or *conflict* and the competent counsellor tries to recognise areas of tension or conflict and consider what is in the best interest of the client under these circumstances.

An example of such role conflict may be a teacher who uses counselling skills in many of her relationships with students. As a competent and professional teacher she pays attention to the pastoral care element of her work with students, and as a consequence develops close, empathic, warm relationships with them. Such a teacher may be perceived by students as someone who can be trusted with confidential information. The ethics of the teaching profession can clearly accommodate such confidential relationships between teachers and students - up to a point.

But where does that point lie?
• Is it the same place for each issue?
• Or is it in a different place depending on the issue, the age of the student, or the type of school?

Imagine you are a teacher in a secondary school. What would you do in the following situations?

1. A pupil hangs around after class and asks if they can "have a word in private." They then proceed to tell you that they are the victim of physical and sexual abuse at home.

2. After a class discussion on contraception, a pupil stops behind to tell you that she thinks she is pregnant and wants to know what she should do.

3. You notice that one of the younger pupils comes in to your class bruised and dishevelled. After class you ask if they are OK to be told that they are being bullied but don't want you to intervene.

Does it feel as though you are a teacher or a counsellor?
What do you say to the pupils about confidentiality?
When do you mention confidentiality?
Whom should you tell?
Do you refer any of these children on?
And to whom?

If you are uncertain about where your primary professional role impinges on your ability to use counselling skills within your role, *you can be sure that the recipient of your counselling skills will be at least as uncertain.*

In Training : Ask trainees to reflect on these matters to enhance
and clarify their ability to use counselling skills as part of performing another role. Ask participants:

"Do I know when I am using counselling skills
and when I am not using counselling skills?"
"What limits my ability to use counselling
skills in all aspects of my job?"
"How do I communicate to clients these subtle
differences in aspects of my role?"
"What managerial support do I need to help
me clarify what role tensions exist for me?"

There may other similar questions to ask which particularly relate to the counselling setting, or there may be a group of colleagues in the work place who can work on these questions together.

If you are able to clarify that meeting place between your job and your use of counselling skills, this should help you in understanding when the role conflict you are experiencing leads you to consider referring your client on elsewhere. It may also prevent you unintentionally misleading clients who come to see, in your empathy and warmth, a person they can be entirely open with *when in fact there are limits* to, for example, the degree of confidentiality that you can offer. It is important that you keep as many options open for both yourself and your client if you arrive at this point.

A careful consideration and exploration of any role conflict you may experience will increase your confidence and competence in using counselling skills ethically, and ensure that any referrals you need to make are done openly, in discussion with the client, and in a planned way, rather than in a panic as you realise you are sailing close to the wind in your professional role, which would confuse the client you are working with.

3) The limits of your competence.

You may decide to refer a client on because you don't feel competent to work with the client for a variety of reasons. Even so in doing this you should understand that knowing the limits of your competence is a clear demonstration of that competence! The counsellor who carries on blindly, who doesn't have any worries about how things are going, who is sure they can deal with what ever comes up, is the counsellor to worry about. Many users of counselling skills will come from backgrounds where the culture is different.

Counselling culture	*Other professional cultures*
No professional facade	Professional 'distance'
Openness and admitting difficulties	Coping and covering up Never letting your guard slip
Sharing worries and anxieties	Being the expert
Being fallible	Bluffing your way through
Knowing your limits	

These 'other culture' attitudes can be damaging to the client in two respects:

1. The client will not experience the counsellor as congruent or genuine, but rather as a 'professional', always giving the impression of 'expertness'. If this happens, then one of the key characteristics of a helping relationship will not be present. Without this ingredient of congruence we cannot create the right environment for effective counselling. Carl Rogers puts it like this:

> "When as a patient or a therapist or a teacher or an administrator I fail to listen to what is going on in me, fail because of my own defensiveness to sense my own feelings then (this kind of) failure seems to result. It has made it seem to me that the most basic learning for anyone who hopes to establish any kind of helping relationship is that it is safe to be transparently real."

Carl Rogers (1967) 'On Becoming a Person' Constable p51.

2. It is clear, and well-accepted practice amongst counsellors of all orientations, that the skilled counsellor or user of counselling skills needs to listen to themselves carefully, and pay attention to any feelings of hesitancy or uncertainty that may be around for them. Such feelings may:

    * belong to the counsellor

     * come from the client or
     * be generated by the interaction (the relationship) between
     the counsellor and client.

It is important to locate the origin of these feelings and this is where supervision can help. (See Chapter 5 on Supervision). You may well get 'warning bells' that ring when you get near to the limits of your competence.

> **In Training** : Brainstorm all of the reasons why trainees may decide that to continue to work with a client is outside their competence. This can also done as a role play of a supervision session or at least in discussion with close and supportive colleagues.

You may decide that you are unable to continue to work competently with a client for one of the following reasons:

• The client wants to work on a particular theme in which you are untrained or inexperienced, e.g. bereavement, HIV/AIDS.

• The client wants to receive counselling in a different arena, e.g. couples' counselling instead of one to one, or one to one instead of family work.

• The client wants to receive counselling from a counsellor trained in a different orientation, e.g. cognitive-behavioural counselling instead of person-centred counselling, gestalt therapy instead of behavioural therapy.

• The client begins to move close to one of your 'tender spots'.

• The client needs help but not counselling help, e.g. help with a housing application or help with restructuring debts, that you do not feel competent to work with.

• The client needs counselling, but also needs other elements in a package to help them. You may need to make a referral to get the other elements in the package whilst continuing to see the client for counselling. Other elements may include medical care and treatment or social work support, etc.

• The client wants a counsellor of a different race, religion or gender. (Although this may not be a *counselling skills* competence issue, it is the client's perception of your 'competence' that you may have to listen to and act on.)

Because of the Client

4) The client needs a package of care including counselling.

Whilst working with a client, it may become clear to both of you that the client does need counselling but also other forms of help, help that is arguably not best provided by the person doing the counselling or even help that is of a technical or professional nature outside your competency as a counsellor or volunteer.

When I worked in an alcohol unit, I was frequently working with people in a counselling way, who certainly needed counselling help but also needed other types of help to enable the counselling to be effective. Some people needed:

• Medical care and treatment because their previous excessive use of alcohol had caused real physical damage that needed medical assessment and/or treatment.

• Help with emergency housing, or longer term referral to more suitable housing.

• Help finding their way around the benefits system to ensure that they get what they were entitled to, or even an assessment for employment training.

This pattern of multiple and variable needs, some of which can be seen as counselling need and some as other types of need, will be familiar to many counsellors and not just those working with people with alcohol problems. To acknowledge the different types of need that a client may have you need to consider:

Can I meet the other type of need? Does it lie within my sphere of competence?

Should I help the client with this problem or is it best dealt with outside of counselling to keep the counselling tightly focused?

Counsellors have sometimes been accused of preciousness and a tendency to consider that most 'problems' a client may present with are psychogenic i.e. they originate in the mind, thoughts or feelings. Although we may hold this as a reasonable hypothesis, it would be unhelpful, and I believe churlish, to deny to any client real concrete, practical help that they may need in the short term.

> **In Training :** Identify all the different types of need a human being may have and discuss which are best met through counselling, and which are best met through other types of help.

It may be that you are equipped with the necessary technical, professional or clinical skills to provide the 'other than counselling' help that the client needs. If this is the case there is an important question that you should consider before supplying this help.

"If I provide the 'other than counselling help' (e.g. medical treatment, social work, educational help) that the client needs, how will this affect our counselling relationship?"

This is an important question, because the different types of help that I have grouped under 'other than counselling' are ways of helping but they are not counselling, and they will look, sound and feel different to the client. If the client is inexperienced in terms of counselling, then the struggle to establish and maintain the equality and reciprocity evident in the effective counselling relationship will be very difficult if you are also trying to act as doctor, nurse, teacher, social worker, youth worker or probation officer to the client. These other roles have an element of power in the relationship that ought to be shared in an effective counselling relationship.

In Training : Consider with colleagues the following different types of relationship that may exist with a client :

    1) counselling
    2) teaching
    3) nursing
    4) being a probation officer
    5) social work
    6) any others from the experience of the group.

List the ways in which these relationships are different from counselling.

Unfortunately the issue doesn't end with a decision to refer the client to other agencies for the 'other than counselling' need whilst still maintaining the primary counselling relationship. Leaving aside how the referral is 'managed' (see Chapter 3, Managing Referring On) another important question to consider is:

"How will my decision to put together a package to provide elsewhere for the 'other than counselling' needs of the client affect our relationship, whilst my prime task is to concentrate on the counselling?"

To some extent the answer to this question lies in what is known as structuring, or how the relationship between the two people concerned is *set up* and *defined*. This notion of structuring not only includes how we open the particular relationship that we're in, but also how we define the relationship the very first time we meet or even before that. (The 'relationship' actually begins before you meet you client in the sense that they will already have expectations and assumptions about you and your organisation from posters, leaflets or by word of mouth).

> **In Training** : Role play a session with a client where you discuss referring them elsewhere for some 'other than counselling need' that they have. Find a form of words that emphasises the importance of your existing relationship with them and does not make them feel that they are being compartmentalised into being 'a housing problem' or 'a medical problem'. Get feedback from the 'client' in the role play as to how it felt for them.

5) The client needs a different kind of counsellor.

You may decide with a client that you need to refer him or her to someone else because they need or want a different type of counsellor. There are important issues to look at here which present real learning opportunities and challenges for the counsellor.

If you feel, as a counsellor, that your relationship isn't effective or therapeutic for the client, there is a great responsibility for you to work out what is going on for you before you decide to take any action. We understand how important the counselling hour becomes for a client, and we know this because they tell us:

"This time's just for me."
"This hour is an oasis in the week."
"It's the only time I get to think."

Even when the relationship feels to us as though it isn't working, clearly the client may still feel they are benefiting. If you sense that the relationship just doesn't feel right, you need to consider what's happening, and the best place to do this is in supervision. It's important that you locate the difficulty, from your point of view, before you open up such a discussion with the client. If you can't establish what the difficulty is, even after supervision, then you are at least clear that you're not really sure what's going on! An honest discussion with a client about the relationship that you have established, and your feelings around it, can of course dramatically intensify your relationship with the client, and it may be that this is all that is needed.

However, sometimes it becomes clear to us, even after looking at the process of the relationship with the client, that the relationship between ourselves, as counsellor and client, isn't one in which the client can work effectively. What is important here is that we get the balance right between

• giving up' on a relationship too soon, forgetting that what's going on is part of the client's process, and

• carrying on regardless, because we know our model is sound and we are good counsellors so it must work in the end.

Good counsellors fight for the relationship with the client; they are also secure enough within themselves to accept that a client may have difficulty working with them as a person, or because of their orientation, *independently of their process within counselling.*

6) The client needs a different kind of care.

Is counselling a universal panacea?

This is an important question for any counsellor who may need to consider whether the person they are working with actually needs a different kind of help other than counselling. In counselling training I often ask students to list the different types of helping relationships that exist, to differentiate counselling from these other activities. Some of the other types of helping relationships students list include:

• being someone's friend.
• giving someone advice, e.g. a doctor.
• being an advocate for someone, e.g. a solicitor.
• being someone's parent.

I always make the point that these other relationships are extremely useful to people, and, I also believe that counselling is extremely useful to people, but that they are not the same. And sometimes one may be more useful than the other.

Consider the client who sits in front of you repeatedly talking of physical pain, it may be that the pain is 'psychogenic', but can you be sure? It's not impossible that, for example, a client sees you following a recent bereavement and experiences physical health problems at the same time, independent of the bereavement. Of course, you can hypothesise that the client is 'somatising' their problems (i.e. manifesting their emotional pain as physical symptoms), and they may be, but if they need other help then that is precisely what they need - *other help.* Counselling can't remove an inflamed appendix, or re-house a person living in poor housing conditions.

If you're tempted to hypothesise about the client's physical or social problems having psychological origins, ask yourself again, "Is counselling a universal panacea?" It should be clear to most people involved in counselling, that sometimes clients will need other kinds of care. The effective counsellor will skilfully and sensitively help the client to get it, not only by making the referral but also by enabling the client to meet and identify their own needs.

Because of your agency or organisation

7) Time-limits.

There may be some factors about your agency's policies that you need to establish with clients early on in the relationship to prevent a situation occurring where the client is operating on a set of assumptions that aren't accurate.

If your agency or organisation specifies time-limits within which you can work you need to establish this very early on with a client during a contracting or structuring session. This enables the client to decide whether the time frame available is one in which he can work. Many agencies or organisations do not specify time frames, but operate on a series of unwritten rules. In such organisations nothing is specified, but a counsellor working with a client for, say, two years would be 'challenged' about the effectiveness of their work. What happens then? Would you end counselling and hastily refer the client on to someone else? Perhaps then is a bit too late to find out that type of limit.

For the sake of the client, and to ensure that your organisation has thought through the issues, you may need to ask a number of questions to help you feel certain that you at least know your organisation's or agency's written and unwritten rules.

In Training: Discuss:
* How long does effective counselling take?
* What are the 'unwritten rules' in your organisation?
* How would you let clients know what these rules are?

---

8) Types of service offered.

Many users of counselling skills do not work for counselling agencies, but, as we have already established, for social service departments, education authorities, personnel departments and probation services to mention but a few.

If you begin to specialise in offering counselling within your organisation, is it just to 'legitimate' clients of the service, or do you have a slightly wider remit, for example including staff members of the organisation? At some stage, if you are successful in defining a specialist counselling role within your team, you will be asked to offer counselling to a client the service would not normally see. For example, you may like to consider what you would do in the following circumstances if you were a college counsellor.

• A staff member comes along for help because his marriage is breaking up.

• The Principal asks you to see her son who is playing truant from school.

• You get a call from a distant University asking if you can see one of their students when they return home at the end of the term.

If you have not worked on this issue beforehand, you may have to make the decision 'on the hoof'. To prevent stumbling

accidentally upon your agency's rules the following questions may
be of some help.

* What are the agency's or organisation's criteria for giving
service?

* Is there a need for the criteria for counselling within your
organisation to be more comprehensive?

* Can I win support for this widening of the criteria for
counselling?

9) Your agency's policies.

Counsellors are invariably enthusiastic, optimistic individuals who
do not fit particularly easily into large, bureaucratic organisations
with tightly worded policies and procedures often seemingly
designed to 'cover the back' of the organisation rather than
provide real help.

If you are working in such an organisation, you may however,
need to know 'local' policies that will affect your ability to offer
counselling to clients. For example, if your agency's policies are
that all notes relating to clients are monitored monthly, then can
you really promise clients that although you keep notes,
confidentiality is assured?

A knowledge of your organisation's practices and procedures is
essential to good counselling practice and good referral. If you are
just establishing a specialist counselling role, and aren't sure of
where the potential conflict lies between how you want to operate
as a counsellor, and how your organisation traditionally operates,
it may be helpful to discuss this with colleagues in similar roles.
The British Association for Counselling has a number of specialist
divisions that may be able to point you in the right direction (see
the Appendix).

3 Managing Referring On

1) **Knowing when not to.**

2) **Knowing when to.**

3) **Preparing yourself.**

4) **Preparing your client.**

5) **The skills of onward referral.**

6) **Professional liaison.**

1) Knowing when not to

The first question we need to ask ourselves when considering whether to raise the issue of referral with a client is:

"Am I referring the client on because this counselling relationship is too challenging for me?"

Counsellors need to struggle continually to develop, extend and deepen their knowledge of themselves, and then use this self-knowledge to prevent themselves impeding the client's process. Whenever you consider, in a counselling relationship, the idea of referral, first entertain the idea that you may be taking an easy way out of a challenging relationship.

Later in this book I discuss situations and circumstances where a counsellor may consider that a client needs help with a formal mental health problem. Some counsellors may considers for example, all statements by a client that are depressive in nature, as evidence of the existence of such a problem, but I do not wish to give the impression that this is always the case. Most of the time, indeed the vast majority of the time, such statements are reflections of the client's process within the counselling relationship. Dave Mearns and Brian Thorne (1988) illustrate this point with an excellent example from a client during the second counselling session:

> "When I'm at my lowest I visit my 'bridge'. It's a high bridge over the railway. I do weird things like waiting for a train to come and then I imagine how my body would look if it was tumbling down towards the train - and I work out which carriage my body would hit...and how the pain would feel...and then the blackness......and nothingness."

> Mearns and Thorne, (1988) 'Person-Centred Counselling in Action', p118, Sage.

To the counsellor this is a powerful and perhaps frightening statement for the client to make and may well prompt some counsellors into making an immediate referral. However, the statement itself is not enough evidence on which to make such a decision. In the example quoted, the counsellor continued to work with the client, accepting the statement as part of the client's process, and this proved the therapeutic thing to do. This being a case of 'when to'.

The decision to make a referral is always at least partly centred in the counsellor, i.e. their personal development, training, experience support systems, confidence and belief in the process of counselling. Any decision to refer a client on will be heavily influenced by the counsellor's process of personal development. Good counselling practice is partly about bringing the hidden into view and speaking the as yet unspoken. The following questions are designed to help the counsellor with their personal development issues that may impact on referral decisions.

"What is the focus of my concern with the client?"

"How do I routinely differentiate between an issue that I understand as a process issue, and an issue that leads me to consider referral?"

"What are the similarities and differences between my decision to refer on here, and the decisions to do so in the previous 12 months?"

"Do I, or does my agency, more often make referrals for individuals of a certain race, sex, class, social orientation than other individuals?"

"Does this client remind me of someone in my life?"

"Does my 'professional background' code of conduct conflict with the BAC code on this particular issue? For example does my nursing code of ethics conflict with the BAC code?"

> **In Training** : Invite trainees in small groups to consider any other important questions that specifically relate to themselves and their counselling practice. Suggest that they list them and after sharing in the whole group, develop strategies for asking themselves these questions before they next consider making a referral.

2) Knowing when to

Just as it's important to know when to not refer on, it's also important to know when to. To develop as counsellors it's necessary to hold onto these apparently diverse ideas at the same time to see the whole picture. On an individual basis, the decision to make a referral may be informed by a whole variety of factors, for example:

a) The training, experience and personal development of the counsellor.

b) The policies of the agency or organisation.

c) Any conflict between a counselling code of conduct and another professional 'code of conduct' e.g. teaching where a teacher acting as 'counsellor' to a distressed pupil is using counselling skills as an adjunct to their usual professional role.

d) The expressed need of the client.

e) The needs of the client as perceived by the counsellor.

f) The advice (or instructions!) of a supervisor.

a) *The training, experience and personal development of the counsellor.*
You may decide to refer a client on because you do not feel competent to continue in a counselling relationship due to your level of training, experience or current state of personal development, after reflection on the counselling process, and after discussion in supervision. This is a legitimate counselling decision and it should feel good that you that you knew *'when to'*. It might be, for example, that you were using counselling skills with the client in an informal, unstructured (in counselling terms) setting. It occurs to you that the client may benefit from a formally structured counselling relationship, with a professionally trained counsellor. You suggest it, the client agrees and you make the referral. This is a client-centred, competent, skilled referral and you were right to know 'when to'.

b) The policies of the agency or organisation.
Another example of a sound, skilled, and competent referral could be where a referral is made because of the policies of your agency or organisation. If, you work for a thematically focused organisation, offering help and information on HIV/AIDS issues for example, and at first contact with a particular client you began to feel that the client may have misunderstood the policies and aims of the agency. You realised the client was seeking general, less thematically focused counselling and didn't understand that your service was particularly aimed at helping those worried about or suffering from HIV/AIDS.

What should you do? If you then discussed this with the client, looked at alternatives and referred on, you would have shown that you knew *'when to'*, and aided the client to get the sort of counselling they were seeking.

c) Any conflict between a counselling code of conduct and another professional 'code of conduct'.
In this case the counsellor may decide to refer on because they realise that the extent to which they can offer counselling as

understood by BAC is compromised by their 'parent' professional body's codes of conduct and ethical statements. The competent and skilled counsellor will track their use of counselling skills with clients and monitor the process to ensure that their work with a client is not moving towards areas of role tension for the counsellor. Where such role tension exists it will affect the helper's ability to offer counselling skills and may compromise any counselling values and ethics. Where this occurs, the competent and confident counsellor will aim to put the interests of the client above any personal desire to continue offering counselling when professionally compromised. The competent counsellor will put the client's interests at the heart of decision-making.

d) The expressed need of the client.
One really big clue that counsellors might get from clients about the need to make a referral is when a client says
> *"I'm not really getting what I want from this.....I think what I really need is....."*
Now that might seem an obvious comment to make, but the reality is that many counsellors may not really wish to refer a client on who expresses the need to be referred on in a straightforward way.

The reality is that such a direct statement by the client does present a challenge to the counsellor's belief in the internal wisdom of the client. There are many views on this issue, but you may clarify your personal position by considering the following questions;

• Do you believe that the client knows themselves in more detail and with more sophistication than you as a counsellor do?

• Do you believe that, providing their world is perceived as accurately as possible by the client, they will move towards actualisation?

These questions are really meant to help you discover how 'person' or 'client' centred you are. If you find yourself agreeing with these statements then it may be that, after clarifying the meaning of the client's statement, both with and for the client and yourself, you will probably accept the wisdom of the client's statement. However, if you find yourself thinking:

"This is simply resistance to therapy," or
"This is really about intimacy," or
"This is a good example of theory X, Y or Z."

Then you may have a less client-centred view and may prefer to take the issue of the expressed needs of the client to some supportive and challenging supervision.

> **In Training:** Set the scene where after a couple of sessions, a client asks to be referred on, then invite small groups to ask themselves:
>
> * "Am I listening to the client?"
> * "What does my theoretical and philosophical orientation (head) suggest I should do?"
> * "What does my intuition (heart and guts) tell me to do?"
> * "What supervision issues are there here for me?"

e) The needs of the client as perceived by the counsellor.
After giving a high priority to the expressed need of the client we might ask ourselves:

"If I really believe in the client's intrinsic tendency to grow, then how can it be possible for me to consider referring a client on as a result of needs I have perceived as a counsellor, rather than the needs perceived by my client?"

An example from my own practice may help to illustrate this point. A client came to me for counselling feeling down and depressed, without any energy or enthusiasm for life. They related their experiences of a recent bereavement and their reactions to this event, which I heard and accepted. However, over a period of several weeks the client gave me other information which, whilst not being inconsistent with bereavement, began to take on a decidedly physical aspect. I eventually discussed this with the client and shared my hunch that some of the client's experiences could have a physical base. I wondered whether the client was experiencing some problems due to an under active thyroid gland. (The symptoms can appear to be very much like feeling depressed or the feelings associated with bereavement.) The client decided to see her GP and discuss this, which constituted the referral on. This is an example of *'when to'*, informed by the client's needs as *perceived by the counsellor*, and shared with the client.

There are examples in many other professional areas that demonstrate how the counsellor may integrate other professional knowledge or skills for the benefit of the client. The point is, however, whether and how to introduce the *'other than counselling'* information without interfering with the counselling process. Or do you think that counsellors should 'hold out' on their clients?

In Training: Split into groups to ask:
* "What other skills do I have and how may they be of use to a client?
* "How can I keep the counselling process intact whilst avoiding 'holding out' on my client when the other skills I have will be of tangible use to them?"

---

f) The advice (or instructions!) of a supervisor.
During supervision of your counselling practice your supervisor may help identify some important issues relating to the suitability of your continuing work with a particular client. When your counselling supervisor advises you to make a referral, you have to listen. Failure to do so would be to operate outside of the written

codes of conduct and ethics covering counselling work, and all the codes covering most professional helping jobs. This drastic step is in fact extremely rare for a supervisor to take and it is much more likely to be the case that you will work hard with your supervisor to prevent such a situation developing in the first place. However if the suggestion is made that you refer a client on, then you will need to know 'when to' and 'how to'.

3) Preparing yourself

You will, at some time or other come to the point in your relationship with a client where you have to consider referring them onwards This can mean many things in the counselling process and your relationship with your client. It can have many meanings for you and for your client. Your meanings and the attendant feelings may not be in harmony with your client's. The referral may be:

• An event that is experienced as very traumatic and disturbing (a moment of loss or grief with feelings of anxiety or sadness), or

• An event that is experienced as in itself therapeutic (a moment of movement to new and exciting possibilities, with feelings of eager anticipation and exhilaration).

These sorts of experience can be seen as opposite ends of a spectrum and it is probably the case that most clients' experiences of referral fall between these extremes, perhaps as a moment of transition bringing with it mixed feelings of sadness and excitement.

Preparing for referral should start, as many things do in counselling, with an inward look at the counsellor's own values, experiences and beliefs about such a process. Despite all we have said about making a referral being the competent, skilful act of a professional practitioner, there is a resilient culture in some of the organisations where many helpers work that tells us: "Do not appear vulnerable", "Never appear not to know the answer", and "Always bluff your way through whilst maintaining a professional facade." Although at a conscious level we may reject these cultural 'commands', such dangerous ideas permeate all of our working life and often impact on our thinking and feeling processes in an imperceptible manner.

The end point of this process is often where a counsellor experiences feelings of failure; failing the client, personal failure, or professional failure when considering referring a client elsewhere, (particularly if the client has referred themselves elsewhere by not returning). *To become aware of such pressures or such a culture in one's workplace may be a first step towards challenging such notions within yourself.*

In Training : Invite participants in groups to focus on a recent example of a referral being made in their agency or organisation. Identify what was said at the time, the atmosphere during any team discussions of the process of referral, and any ideas or values that may have been implied about the whole process. For this experience you need to trust all your sensory apparatus, just as in counselling.

---

4) Preparing your client

If you do think and feel that referral in counselling can be a competent, professional, therapeutic act, focused on the client's needs, then the next stage is to consider at what point the possibility of referral should be raised with the client. For me, the answer to this question is the same as for many questions that come under a broad heading that I would call 'structuring the counselling relationship' - at the first meeting, during any contracting session.

Contracting in counselling is now accepted as an important, even essential activity for counsellors to do with their clients. Some of the focus on the importance of contracting comes from the concern over possible litigation from clients but the main thrust has come with the proper focus on the therapeutic alliance between the counsellor and client. This initial structuring of any helping relationship should not only attend to boundary issues such as confidentiality but I also believe it's important to engage in a contracting process with a client where you openly discuss the possibility of referring them elsewhere.

Most relationships between helpers and people looking for help have an element of imbalance of power in favour of the helper. This is true of the nurse-patient, the doctor-patient, the teacher-student or the priest-parishioner relationships. Counsellors, however, are aiming for a more equal relationship where the client is not disempowered by the process of seeking help. If your clients are inexperienced in terms of counselling then they may presume that the counsellor-client relationship is like other helping relationships they have experienced. This might lead them to expect one in which you are the expert.

A counsellor has to struggle to let the client understand what sort of relationship they wish to establish and that it is fundamentally different from most other helping relationships. One way many counsellors do this is by thinking very carefully about the first meeting with a client and openly establishing a counselling contract so that the client is clear about what is on offer, rather than having to proceed on assumptions and guesses based on the counsellor's non-verbal behaviour, the venue in which the counselling takes place and other unreliable factors.

This honest, open discussion and recording of it at the beginning of counselling are entirely consistent with counselling the values of openness, equality and congruence. It is at such a forum that an early indication that helping options exist, including referral and that they are discussed, considered and negotiated between the counsellor and client as part of the structuring of the counselling process is the ethical and professional way to proceed.

If referral takes place, a recognition of the fact that the existing counselling relationship is coming to a close (if that is the case) is important for client and counsellor alike. During the process of counselling, if it has been at all successful, it is likely a close intimate relationship has developed between the counsellor and client. A referral in counselling is not like taking a shirt back to the shop because it's the wrong size. It needs time, sensitivity and all the skills of the counsellor to enable the experience to be therapeutic for the client.

5) The skills of onward referral.

I have observed whilst delivering training courses, and when involved in supervisory relationships, that counsellors or counselling skills users frequently de-skill themselves when needing to discuss referral with a client. The reason for this seems, at least in part, to do with the notion that we have already mentioned, that referral is seen as some sort of personal or professional failure on behalf of the agency or individual. This attitude can lead to the sort of shame-faced manner in which the issue is sometimes raised in the counselling relationship.

If your attitude, when you honestly examine it, is that you ought to always be able to give the client what they need, then a thorough examination of this in a setting in which you feel safe may be help. However if you do believe that referral can be appropriate counselling behaviour when focused on the client's needs, it may be worth examining the skills that are involved in professional counselling referral.

> **In Training** : In a group identify the counselling skills most needed by a counsellor discussing referral with a client. Which do you personally need to do most development on?

The following expanded list is not intended to be exhaustive. Add to it from your own experience, bearing in mind that the aim is to help you develop as skilled referrers. What mix of skills do you have? How will you go about plugging any gaps?

Active listening skills
These skills such as paraphrasing, reflecting, summarising, linking islands of information, clarifying are absolutely essential in making an appropriate and professional counselling referral. Without these being in place you *can* refer someone on, but not in a 'counselling' way. These basic skills allow for the development of empathy between counsellor and client. If empathy is non-existent, or at low levels, then the referral is likely to flow entirely out of the counsellor's perceived needs rather than out of any counselling relationship and the needs of the client.

Skills of differentiation
This is the skill to separate the issues that arise within the counsellor from the issues that arise from the client. This is an essential skill in counselling referral as without it the counsellor may be referring a client elsewhere for an issue that is in fact their own. An example of this could be a counsellor who has personal issues about dealing with anger. If such a counsellor is working with an oppressed person who becomes angry when focusing on their real experience of oppression, they may misinterpret such authentic anger as a pathological process requiring formal mental health referral. However, if the same counsellor can at least differentiate and acknowledge the issue about anger as *their* issue, referral may not happen or may happen in a different way or for a different reason.

Skills of relationship building
These are the skills of structuring the relationship by being clear with yourself and the client about the nature of the relationship and the boundaries surrounding it. This skill is a pre-requisite for any referral being seen as a counselling referral. This skill is really to do with clarity of thinking around either the use of counselling

skills or a formal, structured counselling relationship. The skill may, when appropriately used within the helping relationship highlight areas where referral is indicated, e.g. a client may come to realise, through the skilled structuring of the relationship by the counsellor that they are looking for a relationship closer to friendship rather than a counselling relationship.

The skill to differentiate between process issues and referral issues. Just when many trainee counsellors begin to feel confident in their ability to reflect and paraphrase the content of counselling sessions to clients, there comes the horrible moment when a tutor introduces the concept of *'process'* as well as content. It's a bit like learning to drive when as soon as you've mastered steering the instructor introduces the need to change gears at the same time! Understanding process issues is a bit like that, in that the counsellor is expected to track such issues at the same time as working with the surface content and considering any referral issues. However, before considering formal referral ask yourself this important question:

• *"Is this something that could require a referral*
• *or is it part of the **client's** process*
• *or the process of the **relationship?**"*

The most straightforward example I can think of would be where a client is repeatedly late for sessions or even fails to attend sometimes. The counsellor who isn't looking at process may wonder whether the client would prefer to work in a less structured type of helping relationship than counselling. The counsellor more familiar with the concept of process may wonder whether the client has some ambivalence about the counsellor for example, or may reflect this behaviour to the client and wonder what the 'lateness' might represent or symbolise in the life of the client.

The skill of reflecting on your practice.
An important element of any decision to refer on should be a close and careful look at the issues involved in coming to this decision,

and the best place to do this is in supervision, or the closest equivalent you have to it, e.g. a team meeting if you're a user of counselling skills rather than a professional counsellor. Without this skill, the counsellor is likely to make the same mistakes again and again, or simply prevent themselves from learning. Of course this skill is more than just having a supervision arrangement in place - it stems from an understanding that to be as good a counsellor as you can be, you need to be constantly open to new learning.

In Training : There may be other skills that you consider are essential before you can look at onward referral with a client. Invite trainees to make their own lists - even a checklist of skills they want to be sure are in place before they even consider referring a client.

In addition to this activity, maybe this chapter has highlighted competent, professional, client-focused referral decisions. If so, make a list of them and decide how you're going to improve your skill in those particular areas.

---

6) Professional liaison.

If you do ever decide with a client that a referral is needed at some stage you will be confronted by having to liaise with other agencies. The only way of not doing so is if you and the client jointly decide that the client will carry out all aspects of the referral. Both the counsellor and client may see this as the ideal solution, possibly (some might say hopefully) removing the need for the counsellor to liaise about the client's needs with another professional or agency. Many counsellors do not feel comfortable with the prospect of talking about their clients to others, given the widely acknowledged importance of confidentiality within the counselling relationship. Our anxiety focuses on trust in the counsellor and the counselling process.

The problem is that many agencies still do not take self-referrals, and it may even be your agency's policy that your workers or only approved third parties make the referrals, rather than the client. If you are put in the position where to get the right sort of help that you and the client have agreed is needed you have to liaise with another agency, then this may throw up all sorts of issues for the helper, counsellor or user of counselling skills. The appropriate time to work through these issues will vary from person to person, but the right time is never whilst you are one the telephone referring your client to an agency just as they ask you a series of questions about your client. It is at this moment of unpreparedness that you will realise how unsure you are regarding how your client would wish you to answer.

Before referring a client on, with their agreement, try to anticipate the sorts of questions you may be asked by the agency or individual you are liaising with, and work out with the client what he or she is prepared for you to divulge.

In Training : Invite trainees to brainstorm all the types of referral a counsellor may make for a client with their agreement.

Add any you come up with to the list below.

Physical health   Mental health
Social services   Alcohol agency
Housing   Another counsellor
Police protection   Legal help
Welfare rights   Self-help group
HIV test referral   Employment opportunities
Education assistance grant, etc.

What different sorts of information may the various agencies, organisations or individuals request?

Even where the client is referring themselves, the counsellor needs to work with the client to prepare them for the very different types of information that may be needed, so that the client does not inadvertently give information that in retrospect they may wish they hadn't.

4 When Your Client Might Need Formal Help

1) What is formal help?

2) What formal help is available?

3) What care and treatment will my client get?

4) The Law and formal mental health referral.

1) What is formal help?

When using the term 'formal', I am talking about the whole pattern of statutory services that are available to help individuals whose emotional distress is so pronounced that they would seriously stretch the resources of any counsellor. The sort of problems or concerns that the client may present with would be described by most workers in these statutory services as *formal mental health problems* or *mental illness*.

Most counsellors would probably not conceptualise their clients' problems, or areas of concern, in such a manner, possibly regarding it as a 'medical model' formulation of an individual's authentic concerns and experiences. I have sympathy with such a view point, based as it is on a *phenomenological* and *humanistic* understanding of humankind. Yet, at some stage in their counselling careers, if they are exposed to a typical client group, nearly all helpers, whether counsellors or users of counselling skills, will work with a client presenting a challenge. Such a client will have a way of describing, analysing and understanding their personal inner world that demonstrates a serious emotional disturbance of such proportions that the helper is unsure how to proceed using counselling skills alone.

When this happens the important question for any helper involved in counselling is:

> *"How will I be able to recognise the signs that my client needs formal help?"*

To explore this question in detail, I will take the example of working with a bereaved person and try to identify what feelings, physical sensations or cognitions that a client may describe to a counsellor. I will then differentiate between experiences consistent with what Worden (1991) calls 'complicated' and 'uncomplicated' grieving, and those experiences that fall outside this loosely constructed paradigm; experiences that perhaps indicate the need for formal help of one kind or another.

The example of bereavement is a useful one I believe since it is an area of counselling work that appears to have grown more culturally acceptable in recent years. My own experience as a Mental Health Nurse and Specialist Counsellor since 1990 has been that over half of the clients referred to me for counselling have an identified need for grief counselling or grief therapy. The well-documented configurations of feelings, cognitions and physical sensations that may be present in a bereaved person are widely accepted by practitioners of different professional backgrounds. It is now also accepted that these symptoms do not always, if ever, indicate the need for formal mental health referral.

In Training : Split the group into two.

Group One. Identify the unusual feelings, physical sensations or cognitions that a bereaved person may have that you would regard as part of the process of mourning.
Group Two. Identify the unusual feelings, physical sensations or cognitions that a bereaved person may have that would lead you to consider formal mental health referral.

On reporting back, compare the findings of the two groups.

In his book 'Grief Counselling and Grief Therapy' the second edition of which was published in 1991, J. William Worden identifies a whole number of feelings, physical sensations and cognitions that a bereaved person may experience that are not indicative of the need for mental health referral. Such experiences, suggests Worden, may fall under the broad heading of '*unusual experiences*' (my italics).

A bereaved person may experience irrational anger towards the deceased person even where the deceased person clearly did not want to die. The bereaved person will often acknowledge the irrationality of such a feeling, whilst still experiencing it. While such a feeling can be confusing and even distressing for the bereaved person it is not unusual. Similarly, many bereaved people experience numbness with regard to feelings in the aftermath of the death of someone close. Even though sometimes indicative of the need for formal mental health referral when experienced by the 'non-bereaved' (especially when pronounced and prolonged), this is an experience that is not uncommon amongst bereaved people.

There is also a wide range of physical sensations commonly experienced by bereaved people. These require the understanding of the normal and abnormal process of grieving, so that a formal mental health referral is not made in error.

The best examples of experiences that a *bereaved* person may have that would not lead me to make a formal mental health referral (because of my knowledge that the person is bereaved) fall under experiences often labelled as cognitions. The particular examples I am thinking of are where a bereaved person experiences hallucinations (auditory and visual) and a sense of 'presence', where the deceased person is thought to be in the current space and time frame, i.e. in the same room. Outside the context of bereavement, I would join most helpers in regarding such experiences as demonstrating a serious disruption in the person's mental health, and would consider the possibility of formal mental health referral, after discussion with my supervisor and the client.

In the early stages of grieving, however, I would regard such experiences as statistically and clinically normal. Indeed, Worden suggests that one of the ways a counsellor can help facilitate 'uncomplicated' grieving is by interpreting 'normal' grieving behaviour as such (i.e. normal), so that individuals do not have to contend with the fear that they are going crazy, as well as having to cope with the disjointed experiences of bereavement.

It is clear then, that even highly 'unusual' experiences within the context of bereavement, do not necessarily lead to the counsellor considering formal mental health referral. If this is the case, then just what pattern of client experiences would lead a counsellor to consider referring a bereaved person for help elsewhere?

Perhaps it is easiest to demonstrate this by breaking the whole pattern of experience into behaviour, feelings, cognitions and physical sensations. We can then look at those elements that, whilst being unusual outside of bereavement are normal within it, and identifying at what stage the counsellor may wish to consider formal mental health referral.

Feelings - Guilt
Many bereaved people experience guilt about the circumstances surrounding the death of a loved one. This is often recognised as irrational by the bereaved person themselves but they seem unable to prevent themselves feeling this way. Such guilt feelings are often characterised by expressions such as, "If only I hadn't encouraged my son to go to university, none of this would have happened." However, such a statement is clearly different from where a client claims that the deceased person died because he is evil, and that he is also responsible for the famine in parts of Africa or the people who died in a recent tidal wave. In the latter example, after clarifying that I had understood the client properly and discussion with my supervisor, I would discuss with the client the need for a formal mental health referral.

Cognitions - Confusion
Many bereaved people experience mild confusion during the aftermath of the death of a loved one. This may range from mild forgetfulness to a complete inability to concentrate on the task in hand. Again such behaviour, whilst unusual outside of bereavement, can be part of the normally expected cluster of otherwise unusual experiences that a bereaved person may have. However, confusion at the level where the client cannot recognise a well-known person,or has no recollection of having met the

counsellor previously for example, may suggest to the counsellor that a formal mental health referral is indicated, or at least should be considered.

Behaviours - Sleep-disturbance
Disturbances in usual sleeping patterns are extremely common amongst recently bereaved people. Such sleep disturbances may range from inability to get off to sleep and then oversleeping through exhaustion the following morning, to early morning waking, i.e. 4 or 5 am. These normally correct themselves in grief therapy, but where such behaviour is persistent and associated with feelings of hopelessness and even despair, then referral may be considered by counsellor, supervisor and client.

Physical sensations - Breathlessness
Clients working through a process of focused grief work may experience physical sensations that are unusual for them. Breathlessness may be an example of such an experience. Clearly the counsellor will first rule out any physical cause, and then, through a process of clarification with the client, may come to understand this as the physical representation of the mechanism of anxiety, often associated with bereavement. If this physical sensation is persistent and particularly troubling, the client may need to consider, through discussion with the counsellor, whether a formal health referral for help with anxiety is indicated.

Other physical sensations
Bereavement brings with it a number of disturbances to our sensory systems and people often develop physical symptoms that mimic the symptoms that affected the relative or friend that has died. It is common for example, for the children of people who have died of a heart attack to experience chest pains. So it may be the case that a physical health check up is indicated and it can often be deeply reassuring to the client to find that there are no physical problems.

The areas of physical sensations, cognitions, feelings and behaviours illustrated above are not the definitive guide to when you might need to refer on for more formal mental health assessment in bereavement. They are simply examples, selected more or less at random, from typical clinical experience and some of the most recent work on bereavement.

It may be the case that because of your specialist training and experience, you would not consider mental health referral where I would. The point of referral may be in a different place for each counsellor. It is important to remember that the need to consider formal health referral does exist for the counsellor working with individuals with a variety of other counselling needs, as well as bereaved people. The most important point of all is that this decision-making moment of referral is unique in each case. It is based on what skills, knowledge and experience you are bringing, in addition to the experiences of your client.

Decisions to refer on should still be taken with great caution as there exists the risk that the inexperienced counsellor, unsupported by sound supervisory arrangements, may over-react when confronted by a distressed client and make a too hasty decision to refer on to formal mental health agencies. This risks *pathologising* the client's grief and creating an *iatrogenic* disorder in the client, i.e. a medically created 'illness'. A typical example is where a client is referred on for formal mental health assessment when they are in reality experiencing only the ordinary, though distressing, effects of bereavement. Such a client may then come to believe that the feeling of great loss they experience is in fact 'abnormal' and seek medication or other help to avoid it. In effect, this prevents one of the key tasks of grieving identified by Worden (1991) as working through the *pain* of the grief.

2) What formal help is available?

If you are involved in using counselling skills, this is a question you will need to ask yourself, and have answers to, fairly early on in your 'career'. Being prepared for the issues that can arise when passing a client on to another source of help can alleviate the uncertainty and stress sometimes associated with it.

> **In Training** : Invite trainees to answer the following question in small groups, then feed back their answers:
>
>   What referral routes are available to me if I am working with a client who agrees to a formal mental health referral?
>
> If you are working for an agency, try working on this question with a group of colleagues.

There is a range of services provided in all areas of Britain as *statutory services*. These are services that must be provided by law. It is useful to have a good knowledge of these services in your area and how to gain access to them should you need to.

When talking about services offering 'formal' help we usually mean mental health services. However, this is not always the case and some services, particularly hospital based services, may still call themselves *psychiatric services*. This is, of course, not merely a matter of semantics, because such self-applied labels do illustrate a particular conceptualisation of what mental health problems mean. As a rough guide, those services that call themselves psychiatric often tend towards a particular model of mental health, usually a fairly traditional *medical model* orientation. In these institutions most mental health problems are considered to be caused by a bio-chemical imbalance in the brain. Of course, this is not strictly true, and whatever services are called they will be made up of professionals with differing views and orientations.

It is up to you, the practising helper, to get to know the 'complexion' of your local provision - who they are, how they work and what approaches they favour. This is sometimes referred to as *'networking'*. The effective user of counselling skills will understand that having 'networked' such services can pay dividends later. The British Association for Counselling recognises the importance of such networking by asking whether counsellors have agreed access to medical consultancy in the papers that prospective accredited counsellors must complete.

The idea of referring a client to the statutory mental health services may not sit at all comfortably with you, yet I believe that the effective counsellor does need to know what is available in case they are working with a client who does need this 'formal' help. You will be a strangely blessed helper indeed, if you never meet a client who needs help which falls outside your competence or remit. What follows is a series of short introductions to some of these services and what they have to offer. Again this list is not exhaustive for two reasons, firstly you should get out and do your own networking - find out the real truth behind your local services, and secondly statutory services are constantly re-defining and re-inventing themselves under different names. By the time this book is published they may be called different things or may have been privatised. The following will give you a taste of what to expect and hopefully help to get you started.

Community Psychiatric Nurses
As far as I am aware, every health district in Britain employs Community Psychiatric Nurses (CPN's) but their role, referral criteria and the degrees of expertise that teams possess vary widely.

Traditionally CPN's existed to support discharged patients from the large county asylums as new groups of drugs alleviated symptoms that had previously led people who suffered serious mental health problems being incarcerated for long periods. Throughout the 1970's and 80's CPN's widened this role and began to work with clients who had not received traditional psychiatric services. Such CPN's developed counselling skills and have often trained up to diploma level, and gained other skills that the new 'clientele' needed. Typically, your local CPN service will be 'patch based', i.e. CPN's will be allocated neighbourhoods and pick up all referrals in that area. Your ability, as a counsellor or user of counselling skills, to refer to any CPN service, will depend on the referral 'gate' of the CPN service, which may range from only accepting referrals from Consultant Psychiatrists through to accepting all referrals from health and social service professionals, including counsellors and often accepting self-referrals.

CPN's will offer a full assessment of the client to establish whether help for a formal mental health problem is required. If formal help is required the CPN can access a whole range of other statutory services and health and social service professionals to provide the necessary input. Most good CPN's will attempt to provide the care and treatment needed, if a formal mental health problem exists, without admitting the client to hospital. However, where admission to hospital is, in the opinion of the CPN, required, then there will be an attempt made to persuade even unwilling clients that they need to be admitted to a psychiatric ward on a short-term basis.

Psychiatrists

Psychiatrists are medically trained doctors who specialise in the diagnosis and treatment of people suffering from 'mental disorder'. Psychiatrists work in teams of two or three, usually with a Consultant Psychiatrist heading the team, and psychiatrists-in-training making up the rest of the team. Although the more junior doctors in a psychiatrist 'firm' are called psychiatrists-in-training they are all fully trained doctors and they usually also have extensive psychiatric training. Psychiatrists usually take referrals from GP's and doctors in Accident and Emergency departments. They will see people referred as emergencies the same day and will make domiciliary (i.e. home) visits to assess patients when asked to do so by GP's. It is unlikely that psychiatrists would see a client referred by a counsellor where an agreement for such medical consultancy does not already exist, though everyone can access a psychiatrist through the Accident and Emergency department of the local General Hospital. Every A & E dept has access to a Psychiatric team 24hrs a day, seven days a week, including Bank holidays and through the night. In a crisis situation out of the usual office hours, such services may well be all that is available to give you and your client the support you need. However, you can expect delays in the A & E as all individuals turning up for treatment will be assessed for urgency, and medical emergencies will invariably be given a higher priority than a 'psychiatric' condition, even though your client may be experiencing a very distressing emotional crisis. Extra support may be required for this waiting period.

Social workers
Mental health social workers are provided by every local authority in Britain as a statutory service. They have a key role, alongside psychiatrists, in applying the various sections of the 1983 Mental Health Act to individuals who are unwilling to receive care and treatment for serious mental health problems, but who are considered by professionals to need such treatment. Mental health social workers working on such legal aspects of mental health care are specifically trained and known as Approved Social Workers.

Unfortunately, the rigorous demands of applying the various sections of the Mental Health Act and the financial pressure most social service departments have recently experienced has meant that many social workers have little time left for other than approved social worker duties. The picture is varied however, and Mental Health Social Workers are specifically trained to work with individuals with formal mental health problems. Referral is via Social Services departments and referral 'gates' have differing degrees of openness in different districts. Mental Health Social Workers can perform assessments and key you, and your client, into a variety of agencies and professionals who may help.

Psychologists
Every health district in Britain employs clinical psychologists; individuals with a Psychology degree and an MSc in Clinical Psychology. There is a shortage of clinical psychologists in Britain, meaning that many departments have very small staffing establishments.

Psychologists who usually take the bulk of their referrals from GP's are trained to assess individuals with formal mental health problems and provide care and treatment for them. Often psychologists will use a variety of psychometric tests to help them to make an assessment. If a psychologist decided to work directly with your client, she/he is likely to see them on an appointment basis, often for weekly half-hour slots, though the exact pattern will be suited, wherever possible, to a particular client's needs and usually on a short-term basis. Most psychologists work with a cognitive-behavioural orientation with clients.

As with Social Workers and CPN's psychologists can key your client in to the different agencies and professionals able to offer formal mental health help. Direct referral from counsellors may prove difficult in many districts, though this is improving as many Departments of Clinical Psychology are attempting to formulate themselves as 'Consultants for Counsellors'. Caution may be indicated for professionally trained counsellors here as such a link-up may become a double-edged sword in terms of the emergence of counselling as a profession.

Specialist, experienced clinical psychologists are highly skilled, and may provide an extremely useful assessment service for a counsellor and client concerned about whether formal mental health help is needed in any given situation.

Community Mental Health Teams
In many districts in Britain Community Mental Health Teams exist which combine many of the professions outlined above and others in a team often covering a defined geographical patch with a single route of entry for all referrals. Such teams are focused on assessment for formal mental health problems and provision of care and treatment to prevent hospitalisation whenever possible. They are often able to access non-professionally trained workers to input 'supportive' care to help clients experiencing a crisis. In the district in which I work, for example, we have Social Services Carers who perform this supportive care task.

Such teams may be a good option for the counsellor to network into as the philosophy of such teams (or individuals within such teams at least) will often be closer to that of many counsellors than some of the agencies previously described.

3) What care and treatment will my client get?

Counsellors need to be aware that if a referral is made for assessment for formal help, the treatment and care that may subsequently follow can be markedly different from the counselling 'treatment' the client had previously been receiving. Although for certain professions that have already been mentioned, notably psychiatrists, treatment will follow diagnosis and be the current 'treatment of choice' unless otherwise indicated. Professions often have treatment preferences based on their training and experiences and these change from time to time. The well-prepared counsellor will at least know of current treatment fads or preferences that a particular referral may open up to the client. Clearly, sharing this information with the client does empower them to make a choice, where one exists, and not to fall unwittingly into the psychiatric 'system'.

The treatments offered by the mental health professionals and agencies include:

Drug Treatment
The group of drugs used will depend on the client's diagnosis. Those usually employed may include:

* *anti-depressants,* given obviously for persistent depression;

* *anti-psychotics,* prescribed to people with a wide variety of behaviours experiences, feelings, thoughts and physical sensations which psychiatrists term 'psychosis';

* *anxiolytics,* given to help in the care and treatment of individuals experiencing anxiety at high or consistent levels; and

* *mood stabilisers,* used mainly for people experiencing grossly disturbed under- or over-activity.

A number of drugs have recently achieved notoriety for inducing dependence in a surprisingly short time. As a result prescription durations are shortening all of the time (e.g. only one week's tablets are prescribed at a time). The distressing side effects and withdrawal symptoms of some of these drugs have spawned a whole relatively new specialism in nursing and counselling, namely tranquilliser dependency.

Even given the increasingly well documented problems with some substances, patients can in many cases, experience such great relief from their symptom that they are prepared to take risks of dependency or endure unpleasant side effects. It is true to say that the care of people with enduring mental health problems has been revolutionised by drug treatment options.

The drug treatments outlined above are still sometimes referred to as 'physical methods of treatment' and counsellors and users of counselling skills who come into some contact with the medical model may benefit from obtaining a copy of the British National Formulary which is jointly published by the British Medical Association and the Royal Pharmaceutical Society of Great Britain and updated every three months. This book is available from any good academic book shop or direct from the publishers. This publication lists various drugs under the bodily systems they affect and most drugs prescribed for formal mental health problems are listed under:

Section   4: Central Nervous System and in particular
sub-sections   4:1 Hypnotic and Anxiolytics;

4:2 Drugs used in psychosis and related
disorders; and
4:3 Anti-depressant drugs.

Although finding your way around this book is a little difficult for
the 'lay-person', when cross referenced with a medical dictionary,
this information can demystify whole areas of the medical model.

Electro-Convulsive Therapy (ECT)
Electro-Convulsive Therapy has attracted much media and public
attention in the past 15 to 20 years. Doubts have been cast over its
effectiveness and it has even figured in human rights cases.
Briefly, the treatment consists of administering an anaesthetic and
relaxant before applying an electric current for a fraction of a
second through electrodes placed on the temples. This induces a
convulsion or seizure from which the name is derived. There are
many reported side effects including most notably, memory loss
and confusion. It is still widely used and is controversial amongst
users' groups and many mental health professionals. It is
prescribed by psychiatrists for a number of conditions including,
most frequently, depression that is resistant to drug treatment, and
certain types of psychotic experience.

Other Treatments
Other treatments that may be offered or even prescribed will come
under the broad heading of psychological methods of treatment,
and although good practice within mental health work is to find the
appropriate treatment of choice as indicated by contemporary
research, in practice in many services, the psychological treatment
offered will be decided by the workers involved and the available
pool of skills in the service:

> *Currently in favour* in a number of services are cognitive-
> behavioural approaches. Many psychiatrists now seem to be
> developing skills in this approach.

Currently not in favour in many services are person-centred methods, or at least not in favour amongst powerful 'culture-leading' groups of staff such as psychiatrists and psychologists.

Whilst person-centred methods might have established a 'grass-roots' popularity amongst some nurses, social workers and, of course, counsellors, it is not clear why there is this lack of enthusiasm for person-centred approaches amongst mental health professionals such as psychiatrists and psychologists. At a time when 'effectiveness' (especially when the word 'cost' comes before it) is at the top of a manager's priority list, it may be that more 'brief' methods have gained favour. Alternatively, it may be a reaction to the demand of this approach that power is shared for effective therapy.

4) The law and formal mental health referral

Mental health professionals operate under legislation that both establishes and limits their power when working with individuals with serious mental health problems. The vast majority of individuals receiving care and treatment for mental health problems are seen at their own request and provided with care and treatment on a basis that disrupts their life as little as possible. This usually means that they receive treatment as out-patients or via one of the community oriented agencies we have already identified.

A smaller section of individuals will receive care and treatment as in-patients on a traditional psychiatric unit, usually at their own request and consistent with the clinical opinion of the professional involved.

A still smaller group of individuals may require some persuasion that they need help, care and treatment from mental health services, but may be open to persuasion from family, friends or other mental health or social services' professionals and will be considered, for the purposes of the law as being 'not unwilling' to receive such services.

A yet smaller number of individuals referred to formal mental health care will be unwilling to receive such care and are not open to persuasion even though they remain, in the view of the professionals involved, including family doctor and family members, desperately in need of such care and treatment. If such an individual presents a real danger to themselves or another person then the professionals involved will consider treating and caring for such a person, against their will if necessary, under the powers of the 1983 Mental Health Act. Such individuals are a small minority of those treated but they do exist and such compulsory detention and treatment (popularly called 'sectioning') does still happen and not infrequently.

Given that professionals working within statutory agencies have such legal powers, counsellors or users of counselling skills need to be aware of the possible consequences for their client executing such a referral. Clearly, counsellors need also to consider the consequences of not acting in those circumstances.

In Training : A useful awareness raising exercise is to get participants to consider just where they stand on this issue. Psychiatric treatments, particularly ECT and drugs can provoke strong reactions sometimes based on personal experience. Don't shy away from the issue, ask:

* "What do you think of ECT?"
* "Are you afraid of physical treatments yourself?"
* "When would you refer a client to a psychiatrist via their GP?"
* "How would you feel if a client that you are very concerned about begs you not to refer them to a psychiatrist?"

These questions need careful introduction and carefull facilitation of the sharing of answers. Many people have direct experience of mental health care, either regarding themselves or a close relative or friend. You may need to have to contain and hold both strident attitudes and very painful feelings.

Geographically focused services
You may now be feeling pleased thinking that you can network your local mental health services for support, but you need to remember that many services are tightly focused on a particular geographical area and will not accept individuals from outside that area. However, don't despair, it doesn't mean if you live in a large urban conurbation that you will need to know all the services in that region to cover the spread of your clients' addresses. A reasonable networking strategy is to build links with a sound mental health professional or service that itself is well networked. Do this by setting up an informal arrangement for 'formal problem referral' consultancy from such an individual or agency. You could, for example, find a local doctor, psychiatrist or clinical

psychologist with an interest in young people to act as the 'Medical Adviser' for your youth counselling agency. They will then offer support, advice and help in making decisions about referrals to statutory services. Most services are themselves keen to network and would, on the whole, respond favourably to such a request. Another good way to start such a process could be during any counsellor training course that you might go on, by making links with any of your fellow students who are in mental health services for your (and their) future reference.

Alternatives to formal referral
I have felt quite apprehensive at times writing this chapter of the book, and this has been because of the incongruity between counselling values and the usual ethos of mental health services. Yet I have also felt that this is an important issue for counselling, counsellors and users of mental health services to address. Put into words the issue is:

> *Can counselling alone be sufficient when we are working with clients whom we consider to have a formal mental health problem?*

It may be worth my restating my own orientation here which is rooted in the Person- Centred Approach. From this, I believe that providing an individual receives the Core Conditions of effective counselling, i.e. *Empathy, Congruence and Unconditional Positive Regard* in a structured relationship, then therapeutic change will take place.

The problem with such a model is that a typical client will spend much more of their life *not* receiving these core conditions, even when in a counselling relationship. This doesn't give the person with enduring mental health problems much of a therapeutic fighting chance if only an hour or so out of each week is devoted to these therapeutic core conditions. There may be an optimum ratio for every individual in particular circumstances, i.e. a minimum time spent receiving the core conditions as a proportion of the time they don't receive them in the rest of their life. Put bluntly, can a person in need of 'formal' help receive therapeutic conditions at a level of intensity sufficient to enable that person to both maintain themselves and begin to move forward?

Some counsellors believe that all clients are 'treatable' using a counselling model alone. In such circumstances we must ask ourselves whose needs we think we are looking after. There are a few therapeutic communities that can provide such sustained contact with therapeutic conditions within a protected environment, but for an individual counsellor, it will almost surely be too great a burden. Whilst it may be important that counsellors 'fight' for their relationship with their clients, the counsellors also need to maintain and nurture themselves.

The ability to command resources to support, maintain and help the client is what is needed, and most counsellors working in relative isolation or using counselling skills as an adjunct to another professional role do not have access to such resources. The trouble is, we often make a referral in the belief that our client is getting access to greater caring resources when in fact they get something rather different, i.e. psychiatric diagnosis and physical methods of treatment. Perhaps, in these days of budget holding and customer-led services counsellors might be more successful in getting access to better resources for their clients.

It may seem that access to these resources is like an impossible dream but it is possible, if challenging to be imaginative about our counselling working practices. Perhaps we could centre our structures within our counselling work around the client rather than the rituals that make us feel safe (i.e. the counselling 'hour'). In this way we may enable ourselves to support some of our clients who may have previously presented too great a challenge for us. Perhaps such organisation amongst counsellors as part of a wider network of helping provision can also free us of the perception that we can only effectively work with the 'Worried Well'.

Voluntary services

Alternatives to the services already mentioned could include the self-help groups that exist to support carers for and sufferers of, mental health problems such as MIND, Schizophrenia Fellowship (see Appendix) and other voluntary groups. Such provision is considered by many helpers and counsellors to be an alternative networking strategy to the statutory mental health services. The level of activity and degree of organisation clearly varies from area to area, though in some areas MIND have produced referral directories, an essential tool for all users of counselling skills, listing statutory and voluntary mental health agencies, with referral criteria and information on the type of service. As well as providing such information, groups like MIND will often be involved in supporting relatively new ventures, such as the Hearing Voices group, a self-help group developing as an alternative to the traditional psychiatric services. Such alternatives may feel much more congruent with counselling values and philosophies than some of the services and agencies previously outlined.

In Training : Make a list, as a group or by yourself, of the non-statutory services known to you. What is their role, activity and level of organisation in your area? How can you increase the scope of your network?

5 Getting Support and Supervision

1) **Defining supervision**

2) **Supervising referral decisions**

3) **The skills of being a supervisee**

4) **Supervision - the costs and the benefits**

1) Defining supervision

Supervision, in the sense that most counsellors use the term, is a relatively new concept to many of the helping professions from which users of counselling skills originate. For example few nurses regularly receive supervision in the sense that the term is being used here, although the picture is improving.

My experience has been that supervision is a widely misunderstood concept mainly due to the fact that one particular function is stressed to the exclusion of all others. This can be illustrated by the following characteristic comments:

> "Supervision is a way to ensure you get the support necessary to do the job."

> "Supervision is a form of appraisal."

> "Managers cannot be supervisors because supervision should not contain any element of judgement or assessment."

In Training : To help make overt any one-function-only perspectives you may have, try the following exercise.
Brainstorm what goes through your mind when you hear the word 'supervision' mentioned.
Compare and contrast your list with those of other colleagues, and other definitions that appear in counselling literature.

Francesca Inskipp and Brigid Proctor suggest that supervision involves a working alliance in which the worker can reflect on themselves in their working situation. This is achieved by receiving feedback, guidance and appraisal. The aim of supervision is to maximise the competence of the worker.

There are key elements in this definition which go a long way towards explaining what supervision really means. A closer look at some of the most relevant phrases will be useful.

"a working alliance"
The supervisor and supervisee act as a team working together to produce a productive working relationship. The relationship between the people involved is the key to good supervision.

"the worker can reflect on themselves in their working situation"
Supervision ought to be a reflective process; a place where the supervisee can wonder aloud about what they have been doing or are wanting to do during their counselling work. However, the reflection is work-focused, it isn't like having counselling where the client can address any concern they might have. Areas of concern should be confined to those associated with work only.

"receiving feedback and where appropriate, guidance and appraisal"
An element of supervision is about receiving comments on, and evaluation of, your work. Supervisory relationships lacking in this 'critical' factor are in reality 'supportive' relationships where no challenge or constructive criticism is encountered and where this does not exist in the supervision relationship there may be an element of collusion, where bad practice can be tolerated or even fostered. The degree of feedback, guidance and appraisal may vary depending on the experience of the supervisor, but its presence will be current in all good supervision.

"to maximise the competence of the worker"
Supervision has as its aim the delivery of the best possible counselling work or use of counselling skills. Its primary focus is therefore not the supervisee as such but the interaction of them with their client.

Other models of supervision have stressed the importance of different functions such as the:
* *educative function*
* *supportive function*
* *managerial function.*

What is clear, whichever model or definition of support and supervision you use, it is 'multi-functional' supervision that is most valuable.

> Good supervision should
> > *educate,*
> > *challenge and*
> > *support the supervisee.*

> Supervision is also concerned with
> > *the Quality Control of counselling work,*

> and therefore includes an important element of
> > *management*

> amongst its functions.

In Training : Reflect on the supervision you have received in relation to your counselling practice.
Which of the functions outlined above has your supervision been most and least focused on?
Has any lack of focus on a particular area been determined by yourself, your supervisor or some combination of the two?
If you work with a group of colleagues compare experiences to help identify any gaps for your agency or team in the focus of supervision.

2) Supervising referral decisions

We identified earlier in this book the complexity of professional referral decisions; it clearly isn't just a case of knowing what's available and picking up the telephone. Professional decisions about referral involve the counsellor closely monitoring their self-awareness, looking at their competence in as honest a way as possible, being clear about agency policy, utilising all the micro-skills of counselling (summarising, reflecting, paraphrasing, clarifying etc.) and knowing what provision is available, to identify just some of the balls the counsellor has top keep in the air at once. To supervise such complex and difficult decisions does require a great deal of skill, knowledge and a commitment to the use of counselling skills as agency policy.

It is the case that many agencies and teams that wish to include counselling skills in the repertoire of services they offer are at the early stages of developing these skills. To insist that they have experienced, suitably trained counsellors to carry out their supervision would kill such developments in their infancy. However, users of counselling skills do still need supervision of their work. What may be helpful is if you decide a checklist for selection of your supervisor perhaps for your own development as a user of counselling skills but possibly for use across your agency or team. Please add to the following criteria that may help you to identify someone able to offer a forum for the supervision of your counselling skills work, in particular with reference to referral decisions.

The ideal supervisor for referral decisions:

• *Is experienced in the use of counselling skills.*

• *Has certified proof of ability to use counselling skills.*

• *Is challenging and supportive.*

• *Is a person of wide clinical experience, including knowledge of or experience in, my field.*

• *Can maintain relationship boundaries where necessary i.e. between their being a colleague and a supervisor.*

• *Is someone I can trust.*

•·*Has a democratic teaching style.*

• *Is able to act in a managerial capacity when required.*

• *Is an excellent time-manager.*

• *Has the ability to be focused on particular supervision functions, given changing material raised by the supervisee.*

• *Has knowledge of, and training in, use of supervision models.*

In Training : Make you own list of criteria based on the definition of supervision and its functions that have already been identified.

If, when looking at the above list of criteria, you realise despairingly that there is no-one in your team or organisation who even comes close to them, don't get too disheartened. You may realise that your agency is at the development stage in its supervision of counselling skills whilst still acknowledging that you have an ideal supervisor who would meet all the criteria you have identified. If your agency will not fund or otherwise support your supervision needs you may have to arrange your own supervision.

You might also like to consider working with a supervisor who, whilst not meeting all of your criteria for the 'ideal supervisor', is prepared to work out a supervision contract which requires them to extend their supervisor training.

3) The skills of being a supervisee

Forming a good supervisory relationship is a combination of the supervisor's attitude, experience, training and orientation and the supervisee's honesty, openness, desire to learn and willingness to reflect on their counselling skills practice. As we have had a look in some detail at the qualities, skills and knowledge that go towards making a good supervisor, it will be useful here to do the same with the other element in the equation, the supervisee.

a) Identifying the counselling skills element of the supervisee's work
Unlike counsellors, users of counselling skills do not always have very clear structures that tell them when they are being counsellors and when they are playing a very different helping role e.g. teacher, social worker, probation officer etc. Because of this, both the worker and the client can be in a situation where inadvertently the primary way of helping is the use of counselling skills, without either the worker or the client deciding that this is the best use of the available time. This factor, special to the use of counselling skills as an adjunct to another form of helping, gives an extra complication to the appropriate ratio of supervision for the counselling skills element of the job. The worker employed as a counsellor looks at last week's diary, identifies the number of counselling sessions she did, consults her codes of ethics and conduct for advice on the ratio of counselling to supervision and organises to receive the relevant amount of supervision. The worker using counselling skills as an adjunct to another professional role may first have to identify how often or how frequently he is using counselling skills.

In Training : Role-play a 'typical' client contact session in your day to day job with a group of colleagues observing. (If no 'typical' session exists identify the different types of client contact sessions first). Ask your colleagues to identify the roles you were playing using the following checklist:

> *giving direct advice*
> *taking a history*
> *praising behaviour*
> *constructive criticism*
> *performing a technical task*
> *(e.g. taking blood pressure)*
> *persuading the client on a course of action*
> *giving information*
> *using active listening skills*
> *(e.g. summarising or reflecting.)*

Compare the frequency of how often you were performing within your professional role and how often you were working using counselling skills.
You may wish to play around with the checklist to make the distinction between your professional role and your using counselling skills clearer for your specific job.

This exercise should help you work out the amount of counselling supervision you need. It may also help you use counselling skills in a more conscious way rather than risk using counselling skills inadvertently which can be seen as unethical and unprofessional. Or conversely you may be performing a different helping role when you think what you are doing is counselling.

b) Being open to new learning
Although I have included this under skills I suppose it is really an attitude that the user of counselling skills or counsellor should

strive to maintain. Given that many users of counselling skills come from other helping roles with an ethos of the worker being strong, perfectly well adjusted and competent in all situations whatever the pressures, being open to new learning, especially learning that is sometimes of a personal nature e.g. learning that you tend to rush in to reassure the client too quickly, can be difficult to take. Such an attitude can go against the grain for many workers in their professional backgrounds, and can highlight a real conflict of philosophy and ethos between counselling values and ethics, and those of the worker's profession.

c) Going to supervision with issues not solutions
Counsellors and users of counselling skills new to formally structured supervision sessions often go along to such sessions with all their difficulties worked out to demonstrate how skilled they are at counselling. However, this way of using supervision time means that the solutions that the worker has generated have been arrived at alone during times of personal reflection. This is in itself an important process for all users of counselling skills but, if done exclusively, it can amount to resistance to supervision. If our clients came to us simply to report on what they had decided to do, we would probably consider making a comment about their process in the session. Deciding on a course of action is clearly an important stage within counselling but it is usually preceded by exploration and new understanding, and this holds true for supervision too.

The supervisee who goes to supervision with a number of issues 'tagged' for exploration is using the time wisely and engaging fully in the process. In contrast, the supervisee who goes to supervision to prove how competent he is because he has worked it all out for himself is preventing himself from considering alternative strategies, and looking at the development of the therapeutic relationship with the client, in a structured supervisory relationship where challenge and support may be given.

d) Developing access to counselling work
One fool-proof way of accessing material for supervision is to tape record all the counselling work that you are involved in, with the client's permission, of course. This may prove difficult in practice if you are using counselling skills as an adjunct to another role, but don't dismiss it out of hand. Properly explained to the client, taping counselling material can help to structure the relationship as a counselling one, and the taping of material can be explained as a means of ensuring the quality of the counselling work, which is precisely what it is. Taping material is only one way (though a very accurate way) of accessing counselling material for supervision. A list of alternatives is provided:

• *Keeping session notes specifically for supervision.*

• *Immediately post-session recording your thoughts and feelings about the session on tape.*

• *Relying on memory.*

• *Taking along to the supervision session, with the client's agreement, all notes and documentation about the counselling work.*

• *Keeping a notebook for supervision sessions with you, to jot down issues as and when they occur.*

Add your own methods to this list, and whichever you choose make sure it means that you can answer the question:

> *"How do I ensure the quality of my counselling skills work?"*

Supervision - the costs and the benefits

The Costs.

1. Time spent out of clinical work for supervisor and supervisee.

2. Cost of buying consultancy support for supervision where the skills do not already exist within the agency or organisation.

3. Cost of training in supervision to develop necessary expertise within the team as a staff development issue.

The Benefits.
1. Prevention of the costs of burn-out by provision of supervision as an 'early warning' system.

2. Defence of 'current best practice' possible in cases of litigation.

3. Enhanced recruitment and retention due to provision of supervision in your agency.

4. Establishment and advertisement of quality standard in your agency.

5. Possibility of applying for practice development grants (where applicable) for practice based on contemporary literature or research in the field, (e.g. in nursing there are Nursing Development Unit Major Grant).

6. Utilisation of supervision as a means of identifying current staff development issues.

6 Developing Your Referral Network

1) **Networking**

2) **How to network**

3) **Networking and your agency**

1) Networking

Throughout this book I have talked at length about the complex issues that are involved in making referral decisions. The issues are more complicated than may initially be apparent and include, amongst other factors:

• a consideration of personal and professional limits,
• a rigorous analysis of whether the decision to refer on is right for the client or a cop-out for the counsellor,
• and consideration of whether the client needs formal help.

At some stage, after this reflection on the appropriateness, or otherwise, of referral, the counsellor or user of counselling skills will have to face the question

"What do I really know about what's available locally?"

This is possibly the most important question to ask once the decision to refer a client on has been made. It would be even better practice to have asked yourself and answered this question well in advance of having to make any referral decision. It is not a question that is easy to answer, and will have to be answered individually by every reader of this book. It is important because, however much you have managed to equalise power in your relationship with the client, and empower them in the decision making process it is in the area of intimate knowledge of other services or agencies that your client must rely on you. His or her perception, accurate or not, may well be that given your role you will have greater knowledge of exactly how other agencies and organisations operate. Your client may have read the relevant leaflet about the agency but may still wonder what they really do and what they really are like. Many businesses believe that personal recommendation is the best form of advertising, and so it is with the various 'other agencies' that provide the sorts of personal human help that a counsellor may need to refer their clients to.

In Training : Invite participants to brainstorm all the places and individuals that you would referring a client on to. Which agencies do you know well and could confidently refer clients to? Which do you have only a vague knowledge of and which would you avoid?

What this issue really illustrates is your need to 'network'; to get to know, on a person-to-person basis, what is available in your area. It will be helpful for your clients, and for you too to have an accurate, up-to-date perception of what is available on a first-hand basis.

Networking is a lot more than just collecting leaflets or information about services. At its best it can mean being a part of a group of agencies or organisations that have different, but perhaps complimentary, roles in helping. Ideally this may even involve a shared ethos that exists in the agencies and can be perceived by clients on contact with the service.

Networking with other agencies can also be an influencing process, where workers from different backgrounds and perspectives can experience the various methods of working and gain mutual understanding and learning. If you believe that counselling does have something to offer, particularly to the more traditional and hidebound statutory services, then networking can open doors to you to stimulate change.

2) How to network

It's important, particularly if you are developing a new role as a user of counselling skills or are newly trained as a counsellor that you actually develop a strategy for networking, rather than rely on a chance meeting or hearsay to find out what is available. A good starting point for such an exercise can be to get a copy of a resource book that lists all local helping services. In many districts the Council for Voluntary Services publish such a guide. Other similar guides are available from MIND who also sometimes publish directories of helping services with a mental health orientation. You could also try your local health authority who in addition to possibly publishing a guide may have an information officer who could point you in the right direction.

Many helping agencies will have regular open days for workers and volunteers interested in finding out about their service, or they will at least be happy to arrange a time for an informal meeting.

Just as in counselling, it's not merely the words that are said that tell you something about the agency or service that you are visiting; the feel of the place, the ethos if you like, can be 'picked up' during visits. Organisations or agencies that are open to, and welcome, visitors are already telling you something about their approach.

Any training courses that you attend will provide an opportunity to make personal contacts that can significantly assist your work, particularly in the context of referrals. If you are new to counselling and trying to forge links for the future then such training events are invaluable. It's important that you make the effort to meet other counsellors and users of counselling skills who work in different ways from you and in different agencies and situations.

One strategy that you might consider to help your networking is to join a British Association for Counselling (BAC) local branch if there is one in your area. Although such branches do mainly involve people trained as counsellors, they will include in their membership many experienced counsellors who already have very well developed contacts. Whilst you cannot *rely* on someone else's networking it can be a useful source of information and a useful starting place from which you can begin to develop your own.

Similarly BAC has a number of Divisions that you might consider joining to meet others who share concerns or who face challenges to do with networking and other referral issues. These are:

Association for Counselling at Work
Association for Pastoral Care and Counselling
Association for Student Counselling
(Aimed at Further and Higher Education)
Counselling in Education (Aimed at Schools)
Counselling in Medical settings
Personal, Sexual, Relationship and Family
Race and Cultural Education in Counselling

Each Division organises conferences and training events, and publishes newsletters or journals.

If your work is focused around a particular theme, and there is a type of onward referral that you are more likely to make than another, then you might even consider establishing a regular informal meeting with a relevant agency to talk about referrals or potential referrals, whilst still preserving the anonymity of clients of course. Such an informal meeting can be an invaluable way of considering referral and finding out about what other types of help are available and how they are delivered, in a context of knowing and trusting the agency giving you the information.

There will of course be many other methods of developing a network. Whatever your networking strategy if it is done well it will pay dividends at some stage when you become clear that your client needs another type of help and you are placed in the situation of asking yourself whether you can trust the services that are available to you and your client.

Networking and your agency

If you work for an agency you may discover that the making and receiving of referrals is sometimes subject to the local politics of helping services. By this I mean that some agencies 'prefer' not to make referrals to other agencies because of their policies, or the reputation of individuals working within them or even rather dated hearsay and gossip.

You may already know or need to check whether there are any unwritten 'thou shalt not refer to...' rules in your agency. You may agree or you may wish to challenge these unwritten rules, especially if your own networking efforts have revealed either that the 'other agency' has changed its policies or that the individual workers are competent practitioners in whom you have the greatest confidence. Such a situation can only result in tension between the organisation and the workers to the detriment of the clients.

It is essential for an agency to have a clear referral policy so that individual workers have a set of guidelines within which they can develop their own personal network of valued contacts.

7 Receiving Referrals

For the most part in this book I have concentrated on the dilemmas, difficulties and anxieties that counsellors and users of counselling skills face when they are considering, with a client, the possibility of onward referral. However counsellors also face possible problems when the referral is going in the opposite direction. That is, when another agency, service or even another worker in their team is making a referral *to* them for counselling.

One of the first questions you need to ask is:

"Who do I take referrals from?"

Many counsellors who work independently take most, if not all, of their referrals directly from the client group themselves, i.e. they operate a self-referral system. This doesn't mean that the questions raised in this chapter are superfluous. Simply that as an individual receiving mainly self-referrals, the issues will be slightly different from those raised for counsellors working in an agency. Also, on occasions, organisations and other professionals will contact you hoping to pass a client on.

For counsellors and users of counselling skills the issues around where the referrals come from, and who the counsellor can accept referrals from, can be very complex. Indeed, if you work within an agency or organisation, how this issue is handled will let you know how close the 'culture' of your agency is to a counselling 'culture'. Generally, organisations and agencies that insist on referrals being made by workers in that agency, and do not permit, or actively discourage the idea of self-referrals have a 'culture' that is different from that of most counsellors. Not infrequently it will be an agency that stresses the 'expert' status of the counsellor and plays down the concept of the wisdom of the client. Such agencies can often justify their policy or restricting the referral path, but underlying this is often the view that clients do not really know what is best for them.The counsellor working in such a culture cannot simply ignore the dominant agency ethos. Instead they may have to develop strategies that enable counselling referrals to be made by other workers and yet at the same time maintain a way of orienting themselves to the client that is empowering whilst providing the prevailing agency 'culture' with a constructively critical model.

In Training : Ask participants to reflect on how referrals are made to them in their workplace. They might try to answer the following questions:
* Are these referral paths consistent with counselling values?
* What does the procedure communicate to clients?
* Is there a type referral that would be difficult to accept?
* How could the procedure be improved, if at all?

However, while suggesting that counsellors should work towards creating a suitable referrals' procedure within their agency where one doesn't exist, there needs to be an acknowledgement that there may be some types of referrals that they would not accept. These limits are personal and professional matters, and are issues to be worked on in supervision, or in discussion with colleagues. It may be the case that, if you are using counselling skills as an adjunct to your main professional role, your professional codes of conduct and ethics place limits of their own. The important issue is to determine for yourself how you are prepared to accept and encourage referrals, rather than have some inappropriate system imposed on you by others who have no real training or experience of counselling skills or values.

The next question to ask, then is:

"On what basis might I not accept referrals?"

The following hypothetical referral situations may help to stimulate your thinking and to encourage you to establish your limits before such situations exist in reality.

Example One
>You are asked to see the mother of one of your agency's clients because the professionals believe that the client's problem may really be the mother's problem. The worker requesting the referral says, "Could you see X's mother, but don't call it counselling or she'll run a mile."

Example Two
>You are asked to see a client for counselling. The worker making the referral says, "Coming to see you for counselling is a condition of the client continuing to get service from the agency; I know this isn't ideal for you as a counsellor, but we have been very clear and honest about it with the client."

Example Three
>A client comes to see you for counselling. He says, "I don't really want to come for counselling but my Key Worker persuaded me to come. In fact she insisted really."

Example Four
>A client you have been seeing for a few weeks about a relationship problem mentions that her husband has expressed an earnest desire to receive counselling as well. She suggested that he come along to see you and he will

come to make an arrangement at the end of her current
session.

How do you feel about each of these possible circumstances and
what would you do in each.

The final question you might ask yourself is

*"If I do accept a referral from another agency or helping
professional, how much information to I want to receive
about my new client from them?"*

Some counsellors like to receive as much information regarding
the client as possible. This information can come in the form of
case notes or conversations with the referring agency or worker.
Counsellors who hold this view may see this information as an
essential first building block in their relationship with their client.

Others take the view that such information is not necessary or
desirable. They believe that the client must come to them
unfettered by the opinions and judgements of others and make a
new start, so to speak. This view is more difficult to enact in some
work situations than others. The prevailing view in many medical
settings is that case notes and treatment notes are not only
essential, but that the reading of them is a key duty and
responsibility of all those involved in the care of the client.

If you work alone in private practice you may well be able to resist
having client's case notes foisted upon you, but you will have to be
quick to prevent even the slightest amount of information being
passed on from the referring agency. It is difficult not to be
influenced by the nuances of a referral that might carry the
message "Please take this awkward bugger off our hands", and not
to 'hear' the almost audible "Phew!" when you agree.

In Training : Since refusing to do something is often much more difficult than saying yes, a role play constructed around the theme of refusing a referral can be very helpful. Afterwards, debrief the participants fully and discuss the issues that have arisen. This may touch on personal material for some people who have difficulty in saying 'No'.

References

British National Formulary, published by Pharmaceutical Press available from the Royal Pharmaceutical Society (address in Appendix)

Mearns, D. and Thorne, B. (1988) *Person Centred Counselling in Action.* Sage

Rogers, Carl R. (1961) *On Becoming A Person.* London: Constable

Worden, J William (1991) *Grief Counselling and Grief Therapy.* 2nd Edn. London: Tavistock Publications

Appendix

Useful Addresses:

British Association for Counselling, 1 Regent Place, Rugby, Warwickshire, CV 21 2PJ

Mind, 22 Harley St, London, WN1 2ED

National Schizophrenia Fellowship, 9 St Michael's Court, Victoria St, West Bromwich, B70 8EZ

Royal Pharmaceutical Society of Great Britain, 1 Lambeth High St, London, SE1 7JN